When B
for Breakfast

When Bees Flew in for Breakfast

Forty original poems for teenage readers

NIGEL TETLEY

THE CHOIR PRESS

Copyright © 2016 Nigel Tetley

All rights reserved. No part of this publication may be
reproduced or transmitted in any form or by any means,
electronic or mechanical including photocopying, recording or any
information storage or retrieval system, without prior permission in
writing from the publishers.

The right of Nigel Tetley to be identified as the author of this work
has been asserted by him in accordance with the Copyright,
Designs and Patents Act 1988

First published in the United Kingdom in 2016 by
The Choir Press

ISBN 978-1-910864-56-2

In memory of my mother,
Irene Tetley

Contents

Acknowledgements	ix
The Prisoner	1
A Year and a Day	4
Trial and Error	6
The Actor's Soliloquy	9
The Perfect Crime	10
The Shock of the Spoon	13
Trewyn Subtropical Gardens, St. Ives Cornwall	16
Colour Contest	18
Mysterious Presence	21
The Interrogation	23
Mahārāja Sampati's Elephantine Question	25
The Bee and the Bat	27
The First Word	28
The Mystery of Inglebrough Mill	30
A Bubble of Perfection	38
The Wind	39
Mutatis Mutandis	40
Two in One (Forwards and Backwards)	43
The Snail	44
The Gathering Storm	45
A Comic Inversion	46
Summer Moment	52
Three Hooded Thugs	53
Puzzling Penguins	56
On the Death of a Friend	59
Wooden Clocks	60
A Question of Guilt	62
Clock Watching	64
Train Ride	65

The Secret Life of the Fruit Bowl 68
  Introduction 68
  I: Fruit Bowl Panic 69
  II: I, Tomato 70
  III: The Fruit Bowl Ball 71
  IV: The Ballad of the Raspberry Crush 72
  V: Olympic Fruit Bowl 74
  VI: His Excellency the Emperor Lychee of China and His
      Treacherous Mandarins 75
  VII: Strawberry Coup 77
Unwritten Letter from a Statue to the Artist 78
The Author 79
Alchemy 82

Acknowledgements

A modified version of 'Alchemy' has been used as the text in a carol of the same title with music by Neil Porter-Thaw, copyright © 2006 Encore Publications. Reproduced here by kind permission of the publisher.

'Colour Contest', 'The Actor's Soliloquy', 'Trial and Error', 'Puzzling Penguins', 'A Question of Guilt' and 'The Author' all first appeared in *Eleven Dramatic Assemblies* (ZigZag Education, 2009), and are here reproduced by kind permission of the publisher.

The Prisoner

Let me out! Let me out!
I am trapped! Set me free!
I am losing my mind!
And I can't find the key!

I know you can hear me,
I know that you're there,
So act! I beseech you!
Please show me you care!

Am I somehow deficient?
Is there something I lack?
What prevents you from acting?
What is holding you back?

Do you doubt my existence?
Am I somehow not real?
Do you think me a phantom?
Do you think I can't feel?

I'm alive! Can't you see?
I have will and intention,
Don't be fooled by the fact
I'm an author's invention.

I have five perfect senses,
I can move, feel and think,
I have likes and desires,
And I sleep, eat and drink.

I have an appearance,
A sound mind and physique,
I'm a full-blooded human,
And, like you, I'm unique.

But I'm trapped in these pages
Of an author's creation,
Living only in print
As a reader's sensation.

I've read books of my own –
Quite a few through the years –
And enjoyed every one,
They've brought laughter and tears.

So I know that I spring
From my author's own head,
But I no longer wish
To exist to be read.

I am tired of being trapped
In this tale of bemusement,
I want to be free
Of my author's amusement.

To be a mere construct
Of an author's mentality
Is to be but the shadow
Of white hot reality.

I want to know freedom,
I want the sheer joy
Of knowing that
I am the real McCoy.

I crave authenticity,
To know that I am,
Just how would you feel
If your life were a sham?

So come *on* now! Release me!
Help me find a way out!
There must be a way,
Please don't cause me to doubt.

For your failure to act
Is now getting suspicious,
Do you think it's a lie
When I say I'm fictitious?

Or have I just made
The depressing mistake
Of thinking you're real,
When, like me, you're a fake?

Could it be there's an author
Who's made up the lot,
And that you, as the reader,
Are part of the plot?

A Year and a Day

Every garden slept in silence
Through the January freeze.

Crackling trees were first to waken
In the February breeze.

Little seedlings stretched and yawned
As the March hares leapt from bed.

April flowers rose to wash for Spring
As showers bathed each head.

Buttercups quickly dressed in yellow
On May's green country hedgerows.

Then bees flew in for breakfast
Over June's sweet-scented meadows.

Borders played with paint box colours
As July drew out the days.

Tired willows napped late afternoon
    In August's Summer haze.

September berries black and red
    Were gathered in for tea.

October lawns were brushed and fed
    As birds began to flee.

November bulbs were put to bed
    In evening's fading light.

In December, woodlands slept and dreamed
    As owls kept watch all night.

Trial and Error

Courtroom eleven was packed to the rafters,
And the people assembled were silent and tense,
For all were awaiting the two closing speeches,
Then up stood the Counsel to make the defence:

"No malice aforethought, no reason or motive,
No fingerprint evidence, no plan and no plot,
No witnesses present and no smoking gun,
This charge is quite bogus and not worth a jot!"

"My learnèd friend's statement is bold and dramatic,"
Responded the counsel for crown prosecution,
"But he fails to acknowledge the one basic fact
That the crowd loves to see a real live execution!"

"Objection! Objection! You must over-rule!"
Cried the counsel appointed to make the defence,
"A man's life is at stake! We must look to the facts!
To play to the gallery makes no legal sense!"

But the judge did not hear the appeal for a ruling,
For the time had now come for his afternoon nap,
The tired ancient judge was now soundly asleep
With his wig slowly sliding off into his lap.

The clerk of the court then jumped up to his feet
And shook the old judge as he snored with each breath,
Then the judge woke up sharply and adjusting his wig
Cried out, "Guilty as charged! And the sentence is death!"

"You can't announce that!" shouted twelve angry jurors,
"We thought that the verdict was ours to decide,
Now you've ruined our fun, there was no point in coming,
It's like having a wedding without any bride!"

"Very well! Very well!" said the judge in confusion,
"The verdict is yours to deliver and sign,
But be warned that you risk ending up behind bars
If your verdict is anything different from mine!"

The man in the dock started shaking with fear
As each juror agreed on his absolute guilt,
And the thought of his neck tightly caught in a noose
Made him feel faint and sick and he started to wilt.

"There you have it! You see? I was right all along!"
Said the judge as the jurors agreed one by one,
"The accused will now stand to receive the court's sentence,
Now what *was* it that you were supposed to have done?"

"I've done nothing at all!" said the man in the dock,
"I've committed no crime! I am honest and sound!"
"Well you must have done something!" said the judge in reply,
"Or the verdict of 'guilty' would not have been found!"

"Can't you think of one thing you've done wrong in your life?"
Asked the judge in attempting to salvage the case,
"For I cannot condemn you without any crime,
Such an act would be seen as a legal disgrace!"

"Objection your honour! I object in abundance!"
Cried the lawyer again in a bid to defend,
"Over-ruled!" said the judge, "We are not in a bun dance!
We are all in a trial that refuses to end!"

"This is a court case," the judge then continued,
"Where no-one has danced, let alone with a bun!
Your objection is merely a hopeless distraction
In a case where no justice is seen to be done!"

"A court case, indeed, where the crime's been forgotten
And where a verdict was reached as a mystery,
But whatever the outcome, one thing is assured,
This case will go down as the strangest in history!"

"And whose fault is that?" said both lawyers in anger,
"For your mind is as dense as the foggiest mist!"
"Well if *I* am to blame, then this case is resolved,
I here sentence myself!" cried the judge, "Case dismissed!"

The Actor's Soliloquy

I am not what I am
And I am what I'm not,
I'm a living and stark contradiction,
I express what is true
Yet my life is a lie,
I'm a fact even though I'm a fiction.
Every move that I make
Is an act of pretence,
A sham from beginning to end,
A sheer fabrication,
A glorified lie,
Whenever I play *Let's Pretend*.
There is no human drama
I cannot take part in,
I perform every role unrestricted,
But alone in my room
There's no sign of myself,
Like a tenant now long since evicted.
My essence is merely
Dramatis Personae,
A bundle of roles with no core,
An identity void
Of a real solid self,
A collection of parts, nothing more.
So when I use the word 'I'
In the course of a script,
What is meant by this pronoun's grammatical span?
Am I me when I act or somebody else?
Which is the mask, which the man?

The Perfect Crime

Three Bedouin nomads made their way through hostile desert
As their sandy trail meandered out of sight,
They had travelled many miles and their camels now were weary,
So the three men stopped to pitch tents for the night.

They built a fire and cooked a meal and tethered all their camels,
Then one by one each man prepared for bed,
And to all outside appearances the men were best of friends,
But the truth was one would soon be killed stone dead.

The victim of this evil crime was one Mahmood Masood,
And on that fateful night at peace he slept,
Unaware that his companions were intent upon his murder,
As one by one into his tent they crept.

The first man poured out poison into Mahmood's skin canteen
That contained his one supply of fresh spring water,
The man knew that Mahmood would surely need to quench his thirst,
Thus the desert heat would bring about his slaughter.

Happily convinced he'd put an end to Mahmood's life,
The man returned to bed without a sound,
Unaware that he was not alone in wanting Mahmood dead
As the second man crawled snake-like on the ground.

This second man crawled stealthily right into Mahmood's tent,
And in his mouth he held a sharpened knife,
He used the knife to pierce small holes in Mahmood's
skin canteen,
Thus draining Mahmood's water and his life.

Then he crawled back to his tent just like a silent deadly viper,
Leaving Mahmood's canteen dripping in the sand,
A dreadful act of murder had been carried out that night,
But the question was by which deceptive hand?

Mahmood's poor dead body was discovered three days later,
He had died of lack of water it was said,
His two erstwhile companions were caught up with and
arrested,
They were each asked why Mahmood should now be dead.

Each man then independently confessed his evil deed,
Which made all legal hearts begin to race,
For no-one could establish who the murderer could be,
Were intentions linked to outcomes in this case?

The greatest judge in all the land was called to try the case,
He was learnèd and his judgements were incisive,
He sifted all the evidence yet only found confusion,
But nonetheless his verdict was decisive.

"As soon as Mahmood's water had been poisoned he was finished,"
The Judge observed when summing up the case,
"But the actions of the second man then undermined this plan,
It's as if the killer had no human face."

"Neither man is innocent, but neither man is guilty,"
The Judge continued wasting little time,
"The killer of Mahmood Masood will never be determined,
I declare his death to be the perfect crime."

The Shock of the Spoon

At breakfast one morning,
As the sun in the sky
Took the place of the tired worn out moon,
I happened to notice
With shock and surprise
My own face
In the back of a spoon.

My nose was extended,
My forehead was warped,
I looked just like a painted balloon
With my eyes now both squashed
And my jaw in retreat
As I stared at my face
In the spoon.

I thought I had melted
In the heat of the night,
(For the calendar month then was June),
But I could not believe
I'd changed shape like hot wax
As I stared at my face
In the spoon.

'How could this be?'
I then thought to myself
As the sight of my face made me swoon,
'Am I still fast asleep
In some nightmarish dream?'
Came the thought
As I stared at the spoon.

But my ghastly reflection
Was quite real enough,
Like the change of a plum to a prune,
I began to despair
And sheer panic set in
As I stared at my face
In the spoon.

I sat there for hours
All depressed and alone
Right into the late afternoon,
When I happened to catch
My reflection again,
But not in the back
Of the spoon.

I saw myself right
In the blade of a knife
And I felt I had won a great boon,
For I no longer looked
All distorted and wrong
As I had in the back
Of the spoon.

I jumped up with joy,
I cried with relief
And I danced round the room to no tune,
My appearance was normal,
I'd been wrong all along
When I'd stared at my face
In the spoon.

But in the midst of my joy,
A question arose
And my doubts then returned all too soon,
Which reflection was true?
The one in the blade?
Or the one in the back
Of the spoon?

To this day, I'm not sure
Which image I trust,
Am I human or a ravaged baboon?
When you look at my face
Which one do you see –
The one in the blade
Or the spoon?

I fear the strange answer
Is neither and both,
Rather like the old man in the moon
Whose face is dependent
On how it is viewed,
As is mine in a knife
Or a spoon!

Trewyn Subtropical Gardens, St. Ives Cornwall

A congregation more devout
Could scarcely be imagined
Than the one that I have chanced upon
And walk amongst today,
Its million-petalled silence
Has the amplitude of prayer,
Giving unbelievers pause to think and stay.

This silence has the stillness
Of a perfect meditation,
Broken only by the plainchant drone
Of nectar-laden bees,
Whilst heady incense coils and drifts
Like clouds of temple jasmine,
As an offering being carried on the breeze.

Tissue-thin white butterflies
Attend both bowed and upright heads,
Like sunlit paper lanterns
In the August summer haze,
Then one by one they flicker out,
Their ministry completed,
As bordered rows sing vibrant hymns of praise.

A counterpoint of colour
Fills the air in celebration,
With the pattern of a richly textured
Musical brocade,
Each tonal sequence brightly-pitched
And harmonized throughout,
In a joyous psalm of rhythmic light and shade.

A sun shower bursts
Unexpectedly and briefly
With the beatific touch
Of a blessing from the gods,
And as if in recognition
Of this cleansing act of grace,
Every palm leaf sheds a tear and gently nods.

This place of contemplation
Is serene and hallowed ground,
More radiant than refracted light
In diamond-faceted quartz,
And the longer I remain here,
The greater my absorption,
Until I am lost within the garden of my thoughts.

Colour Contest

All the colours met in secret
To decide which one was best,
And the winner would be crowned
To make it different from the rest.

The first to stand and speak was Red,
And this is what he boldly said:

"I'm warm, I'm hot,
I'm the best of the lot,
Without any red
You would all be in bed,
For the colour of blood is the colour of life,
The world needs me like a fork needs a knife."

"But *I* am the colour of the sweetest of fruits,"
Said Sizzling Orange to booing and hoots,
"I'm bright-eyed and fun, I'm where marmalade's at,
Without fizzy orange, the world would be flat."

"But what about your fellow Yellow?"
Cried one small voice that couldn't bellow,
"*I* fill the Summer, I am sunny, rich and mellow,
Without my glow you would all be in shadow!
I am buttercup-bright,
I'm banana skin-tight,
I'm as savoury as mustard,
I'm the sunshine's golden light."

"Rubbish!" cried the gullible Green,
"*I* am the colour that you have all seen!
I am mint-clean pristine,
I am cucumber fresh,
More succulent even
Than a kiwi fruit's flesh,
I'm grassy, I'm leafy,
Every jungle shade too,
How *could* you not choose
My rich tree-top hue?"

"Quite easily!" said Aqua Blue,
"For *I* paint the sky and the oceans too!
I have conquered the globe,
I have no need to brag,
I'm a sapphire-cool dude,
With the world in the bag!"

"Oh, is that so?" asked Indigo,
Who stood up tall from head to toe,
"Well *I'm* the stain in writers' ink
That flows from pens and makes us think.
I fix ideas upon the page
In each and every human age,
All composition starts with me,
Long live indelibility!

"Oh do be quiet!" cried Vicious Violet,
"*I* am the colour of a foxglove riot!
I'm the choice of the emperors,
I make men imperial,
For I'm deadly as nightshade,
I am top class material!"

"Hey, Hey!" said Grey,
"We're at the end of the day,
So, if I may I'll have *my* say!
I'm grading, shading, fading Grey,
No artist leaves *me* out of play!"

And then a rainbow turned around
And with both feet she stamped the ground:

"Order! Order! Just you hear
Why *all* of you to me are dear!
In my arc all colours I show,
From red to blue, from high to low,
And *that's* what makes my beauty glow!
So, stop your flap and all your yap,
Just give yourselves one colourful clap!"

Mysterious Presence

I evade all detection,
I leave not a trace,
I have no reflection,
No shadow, no face.

No human can catch me,
No sleuth, spy or guard,
Not even detectives
From New Scotland Yard.

No proof of my presence
Can ever be shown,
Like a criminal lacking
All blood, flesh and bone.

I can bounce round sharp corners
In the blink of an eye,
I can jump up behind you
Or leap from the sky.

I can pass through a room
Without stirring the air,
Then suddenly leave it
As though never there.

I live in dark tunnels,
In valleys and caves,
In haunted stone castles,
In cathedrals' cool naves.

As master of deception,
As genius of disguise,
I can mimic any voice
To consternation and surprise.

That's why you'll never catch me
As I only live as sound,
I'm a ricocheting echo,
Always heard, but never found.

The Interrogation

Did you do it?
Did you plan it?
Did you perpetrate the act?
Do you have a valid alibi?
Or have you made a pact?

Did you think it?
Did you say it?
Has your cover now been blown?
Did you have to use accomplices?
Or did you work alone?

Are you evil?
Or misguided?
Did you mastermind the crime?
Did you act upon an impulse?
Or perhaps you took your time?

Are you puzzled?
Are you frantic?
Do you think that you've been framed?
Are you angry that the game is up?
Or do you feel ashamed?

Are you loyal?
Or a traitor?
Are there values you deplore?
Do you recognise authority?
Or do you mock the law?

Are you vain?
Are you selfish?
Have you courted adulation?
Do you think yourself important?
Is the limelight your vocation?

Have you lied?
Have you cheated?
Have you tried to quell suspicion?
Did you lose all self-control?
Did you mean to cause division?

What is true?
What is false?
Do you have the first idea?
Do you feel that you are in the wrong?
Or is your conscience clear?

Aren't you worried?
Aren't you frightened?
Aren't you ready to confess?
Why don't you just co-operate?
Why don't you acquiesce?

Why this silence?
Why the stillness?
I do not like this at all,
I am Pilate, I condemn you
For a crime I can't recall.

Mahārāja Sampati's Elephantine Question

Mahārāja Sampati was sitting in his palace
When a puzzle of a question spun his Indian head,
So he summoned all his courtiers in a fevered desperation,
And this is what King Sampati then said:

"The ears of every elephant are always just the same,
They are like a thousand winning hands of Indian snap,
But why *does* each flapping ear on every elephant I've seen
Match the shape of India's coastline like a map?"

King Sampati's strange question quickly spread across the country
As the people sought the truth from every Indian seer,
As to why their country's coastline was identical exactly
To the shape of every elephantine ear.

From the sacred river Ganges to the Rajasthani desert,
From Madras to cool Darjeeling to the dusty Jaipur,
From the Hindu Varanasi to the Buddhist shrine Bodh Gaya,
This one question puzzled people by the score.

The question travelled further 'til it spread to other countries,
But the fact was no one had the faintest Indian clue
Of the answer to the puzzle of King Sampati's strange question,
From the hills of Kandahar to Timbuktu.

Until, that is, the question reached the ears of
one wise nomad
Who had travelled over all the world like Indian tea,
He then scribbled down the answer on a piece of ancient
parchment
And dispatched this message to King Sampati:

"The ears of every elephant are shaped just like a map
So these creatures don't get lost throughout the Indian day,
Just as elephants in Africa have ears that make the shape
Of that continent in each and every way."

"That's why, great King, no elephant that you have ever seen,
Roaming freely in your country's mystic Indian land,
Ever seems to look bewildered or in need of re-direction,
For they have the ears to tell them where they stand."

The message was delivered to King Sampati himself
As he lay exhausted in his royal Indian bed,
He then summoned all his courtiers in triumphant jubilation,
And this is what King Sampati then said:

"At last I have the answer to my elephantine question,
And I feel as free and mighty as the Indian sea,
O my subjects we must celebrate with music, food and dancing,
For this day will now go down in history!"

The Bee and the Bat

I once saw a bee with a bat
That batted a bat in a tree,
Now a bat being batted by a bee with a bat
Is a sight quite disturbing to see.

For why should a bee bat a bat?
Could it be because bats are not bees?
Did that bee with the bat bat the bat in the tree
On the grounds that no bat's the bee's knees?

The First Word

The pages of history are littered with facts,
Like who did what where, when and how,
But there's one vital question that never gets asked,
Which I'd like to put right here and now.

What *was* the first word ever spoken?
The *very* first word to be used?
How did it have any meaning at all?
And were the people who heard it bemused?

For who would have known what that first word conveyed?
Without language one cannot define,
So who would have known that they'd heard a real word,
And not a grunt or a groan or a whine?

And how did the speaker know just what to say?
Did he pick on an arbitrary sound?
But how did he then make all others aware
Of the secret of language he'd found?

How on earth did it come into being –
That amazing linguistic invention?
Was its speaker in need of the first ever chat?
Was that the desire and intention?

But who would have known what to say in reply,
Let alone understand what was said?
For that word's pregnant meaning remained locked away
Inside that first speaker's own head.

Was the first word a verb or a plain common noun?
Was it shouted or whispered or muttered?
Just how did the speaker convey their one thought
With that very first word ever uttered?

The fact that the first word was spoken at all
Is a stunning achievement in history,
For how language developed from nothing at all
Is a deep and inscrutable mystery.

The Mystery of Inglebrough Mill

I

The rhythmical sweep of the windmill's white sails
Churned the dark howling wind with the moon's ghostly light,
And the millstones within made a deafening grind,
Stirring owls in the rafters to fly off in the night.

And a shadowy figure hobbled round in a rage
Condemning the oath to which he was sworn,
The mysterious miller of Inglebrough Mill
Who was cursed with the name of 'Troleyfoot Horn.'

His hair was dishevelled and his clothes were in rags
And his skin was as grey as the ocean Atlantic,
His features were gaunt and his eyes were ablaze,
And his body as thin as his actions were frantic.

No person could claim that they knew him at all,
For no one dared visit the old crumbling mill,
He slept through the day, only rising at night,
Appearing at windows with a stare fixed and still.

"I despise every brick of this hideous mill!"
The miller cried out with a venomous scorn,
"The terms of my oath have turned bricks into bars,
All because of the name of Troleyfoot Horn."

"Will I never be free of this half-lived existence?
Is hope gone forever? Was I wrong from the start?
Will the sweep of these sails never bring me release
From the curse of the oath that is etched on my heart?"

This particular night seemed just like any other,
With the dark screaming wind in the moon's ghostly light,
And the millstones within grinding quickly around,
Stirring owls in the rafters to take off in the night.

But just as the wind blew more wildly and madly,
The dimly lit night seemed to alter its hue,
And Troleyfoot Horn stood aghast at the window,
As he saw through the sails that the moon had turned blue.

And then the mill's sails disengaged from the wind
As they slowed to a halt from their clockwise direction,
Then after a pause they all started again,
But the other way round, like a windmill's reflection.

"Could it be? Is it so? Is what I see true?
Am I free from the oath after all of these years?
Is the moon really blue? Are the sails in reverse?"
Asked Troleyfoot Horn as his eyes filled with tears.

Then a loud rapping sound could be heard at the door
Scaring Troleyfoot Horn nearly out of his skin
As he ran down the stairs in a fraught expectation
Barely able to breathe from the panic within.

He unbolted the door as the rapping continued,
Then grasped the round handle and heaved open the door,
And there in the doorway a dark figure stood
In a hooded black cape that draped down to the floor.

In the wild howling wind the figure then spoke:
"You're released from the oath to which you were sworn,
For the blue moon above and the mill's backward sails
Have made safe my return. I am Troleyfoot Horn."

II

The darkest of nights hides the darkest of deeds,
And this story began on just such a night,
When Troleyfoot Horn and his sibling twin brother
Had argued so wildly they drew swords for a fight.

Their rapier blades whipped and cut through the darkness
As the brothers fought blindly in the thick of the wood,
Mistaking each tree for the shape of the other
And kicking up leaves as they leapt, fell and stood.

In the midst of the conflict a voice then screamed out:
"Troleyfoot! Slateyfoot! Have you each lost your mind?
This is not the solution. This is not my desire,
You are sibling twin brothers. You are two of a kind."

"It is I, your Cordelia! Don't you hear what I say?
I beseech you to stop! Each now lay down your sword!"
But Cordelia's voice made each man fight the harder,
Inflicting worse wounds from which a brother's blood poured.

Then in the confusion of anger and darkness,
Both swords locked together and combined for the kill,
As they swung in an arc and pierced the soft body
Of the lovely Cordelia who fell silent and still.

Cordelia fell barely able to breathe
In her white linen dress stained dark red with her blood,
And for one dreadful moment the universe stopped
As the brothers both dropped to their knees in the mud.

Troleyfoot Horn and his twin brother Slateyfoot
Held Cordelia gently as they knelt at her side,
They had fought for her love, not her untimely death,
Now they begged for forgiveness and like children they cried.

"You have always been enemies since the day you were born,"
Cordelia spluttered with a faltering voice,
"You are sibling twin brothers, yet you live as dark rivals,
But in these last words to you, I give you this choice."

"If you want my forgiveness you must put out the fire
Of the hatred that has burnt in your lives from the start,
You must learn what it means to become one another,
Only then will you feel what is in your twin's heart."

"My last dying wish is to hear you both swear
That from now you will live as each other's reflection,
By exchanging your names, your lives and personas,
Thus replacing dark hatred with fraternal affection."

"We give you our word. What you wish we shall do,"
Sobbed each of the brothers, each one now a killer,
"Troleyfoot shall from now on be the soldier,
And the once-soldier Slateyfoot shall from now be the miller."

"Thus it shall be," said Cordelia weakly,
"Thus shall you live until two signs appear,
Two wonderful signs that will signal release
From the terms of your oath and the guilt that you fear."

"When the windmill's white sails disengage from the wind
And the moon in the sky turns from grey into blue,
Shall be the two signs that ensure your reunion
As brothers, not rivals, and I then to you."

"What do you mean when you say 'I to you'?"
The brothers both asked but to no end or good,
For Cordelia died in their arms on the ground
On that darkest of nights, in the heart of the wood.

III

And so we return to where we began,
With the once warring brothers united once more,
Released from the oath they had sworn to Cordelia
On that darkest of nights, a half century before.

The sibling twin brothers had been true to their word
For fifty long years since that terrible night,
The one was confined to Inglebrough Mill,
The other to far-distant countries to fight.

And they never forgot poor Cordelia's words,
For each night they would stare at the moon up above
In the hope it would turn its grey light into blue,
Thus undoing the oath both had sworn out of love.

Until the events of that wonderful night
When the tired worn out moon did indeed turn bright blue
And the windmill's white sails disengaged from the wind
To signal Cordelia's words had come true.

But over the years, those fifty long years,
Each brother became his lost sibling's reflection
As the hatred between them diminished and faded,
And in its place grew a fraternal affection.

And behind the stone walls of Inglebrough Mill,
The sibling twin brothers talked right through the night,
Relating their stories of fifty years past
With laughter and tears in the moon's pure blue light.

They remembered with anguish Cordelia's death
And her final five words: 'And I then to you,'
And Troleyfoot asked, "What *did* those words mean?
They defy explanation. How could they be true?"

"I agree, my dear brother, they have haunted my nights,"
Said Slateyfoot wiping away a lone tear,
"But all else that she said has come true on this night,
We *must* not lose faith, I feel she is near."

****

The following morning, a cold winter sun
Shone like counterfeit gold over Inglebrough Mill,
The windmill's four sails were frozen and dormant,
The millstones within lay eerily still.

Inglebrough Mill was empty and silent,
Of the night's strange events not a trace could be found,
The sibling twin brothers had gone like a dream,
And nothing was left – neither shadow nor sound.

The silence was broken by the sound of three children
Running over the fields to where the mill stood,
Twin boys with a girl in a white linen dress
Who had spent all the morning playing games in the wood.

The boys were competing for who could run faster,
While the girl lagged behind nearly out of her breath,
But she just about managed to call after each brother:
"Please both of you stop, or you'll run me to death!"

They ran past the mill in search of adventure,
But when they had gone, the air started to churn,
First a mild gentle breeze, then a wild screaming gale,
And the windmill's white sails slowly started to turn.

A Bubble of Perfection

Nothing is as perfect as a bubble,
A faulty bubble simply cannot be,
You will never find a bubble
That is dented, scratched or broken,
Such an apparition you will never see.

Mathematically a bubble is unequalled,
Its surface is a geometric wonder,
It's as infinite in tangents
As identical in angles,
This is $4\pi r^2$ without a blunder.

Its curvature is absolute exactitude,
An equi-balanced sphere of pure delight,
As elusive as a shadow,
And as fragile as a prayer,
Or an uncorrupted thought that's taken flight.

The beauty of a bubble can't be captured,
When plotted on the axes: x, y, z,
Its co-ordinates are endless,
It defies full definition,
Like the meaning of a word that can't be said.

A bubble can exist in air or liquid,
Drifting down or gently floating to the top,
But this happy ball of fun
Has a hidden tragic nature,
For just as it gets going, it goes POP!

The Wind

Like a ghost, the wind lives as an absence,
Existing as barely a trace,
Like an opera without composition,
Or a portrait without any face.

Like a weaver it threads up and under,
Entwining the warp with the weft,
But so deftly in skill and precision
That only the movement is left.

It can scream like a menacing banshee,
Without larynx or tongue it can cry
As it visits dark violence upon you
From the threat of a cloud-blackened sky.

It can move without muscle or sinew
Gymnastic in power and grace,
At a pitch of athletic performance
Where nothing remains but the race.

Like the sweep of a mesmerised dervish,
It can whirl in a torrent of twists
With such furious frenzied momentum,
That the dancer no longer exists.

The wind rushes onward from nowhere,
To an end-point that reaches no rest
As it swells like the turbulent ocean,
But its waves have no trough and no crest.

Only nothing can come out of nothing,
So how does the wind gain its force?
Is the wind an exception of nature?
Is nothing the wind's hidden source?

Mutatis Mutandis

Mutatis and Mutandis were identical twin brothers
Who always went round back to back which always baffled others.
You could not tell the two apart, their sameness was perfection,
Except they always faced in quite the opposite direction.

Now Mutatis and Mutandis had a very cunning streak,
Each took a turn at telling lies on different days each week,
As one told lies the whole day long, the other told the truth,
But the next day they would swap right round, it really was uncouth.

The challenge they presented was to prove which one was lying,
But all had failed to foil their game, though not through lack of trying,
For every time a question was addressed to either brother,
Each one would widely grin and say the liar was the other.

Until that is they went to court on charges of deception
Where a judge gave each a quizzical and sceptical reception,
The brothers shook and trembled as they stood there in the dock,
Their game had gone too far and now their heads were on the block.

"Mutatis and Mutandis!" said the Judge with piercing eyes,
"How many of you here today are telling only lies?"
Mutatis looked up meekly and declared: "There's one at least!"
"Don't believe him!" said Mutandis, "He's a dirty lying beast!"

"Enough! I've solved the riddle of your ghastly little game!"
Said the Judge as he considered how to allocate the blame.
"With a simple direct question, I prepared a deadly trap,
And you, Mutandis, fell right in. Now feel its jaws go snap!"

"If Mutatis is the liar, then his statement is not true,
But that would mean that no-one's lying – neither he nor you –
Yet such a situation is impossibly absurd,
So Mutandis, it is *you* who lies with every spoken word!"

Mutatis and Mutandis started crying floods of tears,
Their game had been undone which they'd enjoyed
for many years,
The Judge then passed his sentence on each brother in the dock,
And they both began to wish that they could turn
back every clock.

"Your sentence is decided!" said the Judge whose
voice went deep,
"But you'll each receive a different one and each is
yours to keep."
Each brother then received a piece of paper double-sided,
And on each one was written down the sentence so-decided.

The first one read: *Your brother's sentence is a total lie.*
And as Mutatis read it out he wondered how and why,
Then Mutandis read *his* sentence out and found it said forsooth:
Your brother's single sentence is undoubtedly the truth.

In attempting to work out which of their sentences was true,
The brothers started fighting as they hadn't got a clue,
The twins had now been given what they'd meted out to others,
Which meant that no-one else again was bothered by those brothers.

Two in One
(Forwards and Backwards)

.ODD, QUITE, ARE THEY THAT THINK *WILL YOU?*

,STRANGE, TOO, ARE THEY THAT THINK *MIGHT YOU?*

!GOD-LIKE ARE THEY THAT THINK *DARE YOU!*

,MISGUIDED ARE THEY THAT THINK *CAN YOU?*

The Snail

I'm a slowly moving mollusc
With a single slimy foot,
I'm as slippery as an oil slick,
But my shell is dry as soot.

I leave a sticky silvery trail
Wherever I choose to roam,
But my shell makes me ungainly,
It's my constantly mobile home.

I dine on lettuce lightly dressed
In the cool vinaigrette of the rain,
Which is why every farmer regards me
As a foul horticultural pain.

It is not only birds that consume me,
To the French I'm a delicate starter,
But the Jews find me not at all kosher,
For their faith has a snail-friendly charter.

Because of my moist constitution,
Salinity catches my breath,
Which is why wicked children attack me
With salt which quite foams me to death.

But as for my moments of romance,
They're a secret I never will tell,
For the mere thought of broaching this subject
Makes me shyly withdraw to my shell.

The Gathering Storm

We ignored every signal and warning
In the haze of that high Summer heat,
Our lives had become rich and easy
With the wealth of the world at our feet.

We thought it would go on for ever,
That slow lazy jazz riff of Summer,
But a vast distant army had gathered,
Marching straight to the beat of a drummer.

Battalions moved in formation
And blackened the rolling terrain,
Their advancement was swift and relentless
With an anger no force could constrain.

The first shots were fired at a distance,
Wild flashes preceding the thunder,
A menacing threat was upon us
And the ease of our lives tore asunder.

Munitions rained down on our heads
In that terrible one-sided fight,
We retreated to a state of besiegement
As hope petered out with the light.

The onslaught continued for days
And after the tempestuous campaign,
We felt a cold chill as our dreams lay in ruins,
The Winter was ours once again.

A Comic Inversion

Four royal Houses had reigned throughout all human history,
Four dynastic bloodlines – the origins of which were a mystery.

Four regal lineages – each like an unbroken thread,
Four families majestic – two heraldically black and two red.

These four imperial Houses were patrons of the Gambling Arts:
The Houses of Clubs and Spades and the Houses of Diamonds and Hearts.

They were equal in status and power and also in family size,
Each household consisted of thirteen relations bound firmly by family ties.

Together these sovereign Houses were served by two mischievous Jesters
Who flitted between all four Houses as buffooning and joking contesters.

But these Jesters were up to no good, for they'd hatched a dastardly plan
Of causing confusion and mayhem as only two harlequins can.

They requested an audience-royal which was granted the very same day,
And with fifty-two royals assembled, their plan was now well under way.

* *

"If you've got the pigeons, then we've got the cat!"
Said the Jesters with menacing humour,
"For we've gleaned a harsh fact from the World of the Players
That is not speculation or rumour."

"We do not have pigeons any more you've a cat,"
Said the Red King of Hearts standing tall,
"Remember your place, you impertinent fools!
Speak plainly, or don't speak at all!"

"Yes – *what* is this fact that you speak of?"
Asked the King of Clubs swinging his sword,
"It must be important, so cut the suspense!
We royals are easily bored."

"It would seem a decision's been taken, just so,"
Said the Jesters both stifling laughter,
"To establish a new royal House, yes indeed,
And kill off one of yours ever after!"

There were shrieks, loud gasps and sharp intakes of breath
As the shock of this news shook each royal,
And the Jesters perversely took utter delight
In the fact they had been so disloyal.

"Grill a moth as it gnaws through a rafter?
Is that what I heard someone say?"
Said the Red King of Diamonds awaking
Who 'til now had been sleeping all day.

"And what is the name of this new royal House?"
Asked the Queen of Spades cutting him short,
"The name of this House is 'Emanon', ma'am,"
Came the Jesters quick-thinking retort.

"Emanon? Emanon? The royal House of Emanon?
What a ghastly ridiculous name!"
Cried the four Knaves in chorus with moustaches
now twitching
With anger that burned like a flame.

The Red King of Diamonds was still half asleep
And mishearing each word that was said,
'til the Black Queen of Clubs cried with anger and bile,
"Well, there's one king who's practically dead!"

"How dare you insult my dear husband!"
Said the Red Queen of Diamonds in tears,
"My husband is frail and exhausted and weak
And advanced in his age by some years."

"We're in deep constitutional crisis
And all he can do is just sleep,"
The King of Clubs said just to follow his wife
As he always did just like a sheep.

"Yes, it must be the Diamonds' red bloodline
That the Players intend to replace,
Such a tired worn out king is no use to the World,"
Said the King of Spades stroking his mace.

"What makes you so sure *your* two Houses are safe?"
Warned the Red Queen of Hearts with a roar,
"For everyone knows that all dark evil deeds
Have a Club and a Spade at their core."

"You impugn our Houses with slanderous lies!
Forgetting *your* criminal past,
Of the case of your Knave who stole all of the tarts,"
The King of Clubs preened to the last.

"That was a court case intended as fiction,"
Said the King of Hearts backing his son,
"The case was invention – a sheer fabrication –
Nothing more than mere fairy tale fun."

"Tell that to the Players as they cut your red bloodline!"
The Queen of Spades boomed to coarse laughter,
"For smoke never rises without any fire
And mud always sticks ever after!"

An argument-royal was now in full flood
As each House tried to safeguard its status,
Accusations were flying both backward and forward
With no prospect in sight of hiatus.

So fierce was the battle that nobody noticed
The Jesters both rolling with mirth on the floor,
Their behaviour was mad, and as crude and as daft
As the three-pointed floppy felt hats that they wore.

And the poor King of Diamonds had gone back to sleep,
Right back to the world that he dreamed,
For now he was talking aloud as he slept,
Both forwards and backwards it seemed.

Each word that he spoke, he repeated just once,
In a style that was strangely compelling,
For each repetition he pronounced in reverse,
Like an echo inverting the spelling.

'Cat' became 'tac' and 'milk' became 'klim'
As each word took a different direction,
Whatever the dream, it was causing the King
To perceive every word in reflection.

His curious mumblings grew louder and louder,
So much so that the arguing ceased,
The squabbling royals were shocked into silence
As the King's strange inversions increased.

"He's gone out of his mind!" said the Black Queen of Clubs
As the Diamond King rambled and rambled,
"He has lost all his wits!" said the Red King of Hearts,
"His mind is like egg that's been scrambled!"

The King's fretful wife started mopping his brow
For fear that the King was delirious,
"All this fighting has upset his balance of mind,"
Said the Queen in a tone deadly serious.

The Jesters' ridiculous laughter continued
Right in front of them all from the Kings to the Aces,
But the sound of the next word the Diamond King uttered
Wiped the smiles off their silly red faces.

"EMANON!" shouted the Red King of Diamonds,
And the Jesters' wild mirth turned to shame,
For they knew that the next words would be their undoing
As the King loudly shouted, "NO NAME!"

"Emanon, No name?" the Knaves said in chorus,
As truth struck each one like a Muse,
"Have the Jesters deceived us with mischievous lies?
Is this whole thing a harlequin's ruse?"

"The royal House of Emanon simply does not exist!
This House is a phantom, a lie and a fake!
Explain yourselves, Jesters!" the Knaves then demanded,
When the Red Diamond King sharply sat up awake.

"We made it all up," both Jesters said meekly,
"We thought it a jest, now the joke lies in shards,
The Emanon House has no basis in fact,
It was from the outset a mere house of cards."

"A mere house of cards!" the Diamond King chortled,
"How supremely bizarre! How sublimely absurd!
What a fabulous trick of a double-edged meaning!
That's the funniest answer that I've ever heard!"

The fifty-two royals then one after the other
Started giggling and laughing – every adult and child –
For they should have suspected a comic inversion,
After all, of all cards, only Jokers are wild!

Summer Moment

Two tissue-thin white butterflies gently flutter in the haze,
As flakes of ash arising from the Summer's bonfire blaze.

Three Hooded Thugs

They broke in all at once,
And nobody bothered to raise the alarm,
Three hooded thugs
Broke into a house
Where a decent man lived
Who they wanted to harm.

They dragged him
And mocked him,
They punched him
And kicked him,
They ransacked his house
And left not a trace,
They took all they wanted
And smashed up the rest,
Then as they were leaving,
They spat in his face.

"Why have you done this?
Who *are* you? Tell me!"
The broken man said
As they made for the door,
The three thugs then stopped
And turned back to the man
As he lay in the debris
Dashed with blood on the floor.

The first thug stepped forward
And took off his hood,
"I am Illness," he said,
"Your decline is my gain,
Every seizure and ache,
Every nauseous moment,
Every long sleepless night,
Every fever and chill,
Every shortness of breath,
Every chronic discomfort,
Is a blow I've delivered
Again and again."

"And I am Old Age,"
The second thug stuttered,
"In this bag on my shoulder
I've got your whole past,
Your youthful appearance,
Your purpose and status,
The spring in your step
And your quicksilver mind,
I tell you these things
I have taken for ever,
Your life is now mine
From the first to the last."

"Not quite," said the last thug,
"There is still something left,
And that now is mine,
For my name is Death,
I have taken already
Your friends and your loved ones,
Your skills and your talents,
Your hopes and your dreams,
But now it is time
To finish you off,
To take what remains:
Your last human breath."

They trooped out one by one,
(And still no one bothered to raise the alarm,)
Three hooded thugs
Had taken the life
Of a man who had done
Not the slightest of harm.

Puzzling Penguins

Two penguins called Olly and Joe
Both lived in the cold arctic snow,
They talked and they fished,
And they ate all they wished,
Then off to their beds they would go.

And each night was exactly the same,
When they'd play a most difficult game
Of each asking a question
For mental digestion,
Where no answer was always the aim.

Now Olly was desperate to win,
And his mind was as sharp as a pin,
So he started to question
Without much suggestion,
As Joe scratched his head and his chin.

"Now where does the sun go at night?
And what gives the moon its grey light
When the sky is as black
As a coalminer's sack,
And the sun is just nowhere in sight?"

"And why when you pull out the plug,
Which hangs on a chain that you tug,
Does the water swirl round
As it flows underground,
When it always flows straight from a jug?"

"While I'm speaking of water's strange action,
I'll ask about liquid subtraction,
Rivers pour in the sea
Like a cup fills with tea,
Yet the sea never rises a fraction."

"And then there's the question of hue,
Like if everyone sees the same blue,
When we look at the skies
With our own different eyes,
Do I see the same colour as you?"

"Now what does it mean when you hear,
'We're the same through each day, month and year'?
Is a tadpole the frog?
Is an adult the sprog?
What we are is not totally clear."

"But it's the question of clocks that you'll hate,
With their pendulums, bells and true date,
Before their invention
By men of convention,
Was anyone then ever late?"

"And then there's the question of God,
Whose power always strikes me as odd,
For could God make a stone
Of such weight he alone
Could not lift it with pulley or rod?"

"Now a tree that falls down to the ground,
Makes a crash like a drum that you pound,
But if no-one is there
As it falls through the air,
Could you say that the tree makes a sound?"

"Enough now! Enough!" cried poor Joe,
"Your questions have struck quite a blow,
It's my turn to ask *you*
A trick question or two
So be still and let *me* have a go!"

"Are we part of a dwindling race –
Us two penguins up here in this place?
Why are we alone
In this north arctic zone?
Have all penguins run off without trace?

"Your question's no puzzle or trick!"
Said Olly, the clever old stick,
"For penguins aren't found
 On the north arctic ground,
But only down south in Antarctic!"

On the Death of a Friend

Don't mention his name,
Don't speak of the past,
I need no reminding
That nothing can last.

Indulge me with small-talk
When you drop by or call,
Please help me pretend
To feel nothing at all.

Put away all the photos,
Each album and book,
Let me live on the surface,
Do not force me to look.

Disregard my despair
And ignore every tear
When in moments of madness
I think he's still here.

Convince me I'm foolish,
Turn my heart into stone,
Extinguish my grief,
Or else leave me alone.

He was only a dog,
A mere pet by design,
(But this dog was a friend,
He was loved, he was mine.)

Wooden Clocks

Imagine a clock without any face,
Without any numbers or date,
No minute hand, hour hand,
No mechanical cogs,
No slow swinging pendulum weight.

Such featureless clocks are readily found
In a woodland or forest or glade,
They have twiglets and bark,
Thick branches and roots,
They have leaves, each one coloured like jade.

As the Earth spins and orbits
A gyroscope sun,
The seasons arise in a round,
A planetary carousel, endless and vast,
By which trees keep the time from the ground.

These wooden chronometers start in the Spring
When sunshine and rain both appear in a flash,
When Winter's harsh patterns
Of filigree branches
Are shattered by buds breaking out like a rash.

Summer heat waves bring forth an outward profusion
Of foliage uniform in shape and design,
A green calibration
Marked out on each twig,
Nature's timepiece is never so wondrously fine.

Autumn days then wind down in a weakening sun
And dry brittle leaves curl and drift to the ground
As physical seconds,
Falling markers of time,
As an hourglass upturned, moments pass without sound.

With one annual cycle quite fully completed,
The world is now aged by a single degree
And a record is made
Of this one revolution
By adding the same to the trunk of each tree.

A Question of Guilt

The kangaroo stood in the dock of the court
For a very marsupial crime,
She'd been found with a pocket-watch tucked in her pouch,
When a mongoose had asked her the time.

"Misuse of the pouch is a breach of the law,"
Said the judge as he brought her to book,
"The verdict of guilty means only one thing,
You're an evil marsupial crook!"

The kangaroo took great exception to this
And wanted to start an affray,
But she gathered herself and addressed the old judge:
"Your Honour! I've something to say!"

"You clearly believe I'm inherently bad,
On the grounds that I've broken the law,
But I put it to you that your judgement is wrong,
Your belief has a logical flaw."

"How so?" said the judge, now quite taken aback
At the shock of this bold contradiction,
"Present me with proof that my judgement is wrong,
Or I'll hand down a double conviction!"

The kangaroo took up the challenge at once:
"Your Honour, please listen, I beg!
To say that my guilt means my character's bad
Is a clear case of chicken and egg!"

"Am I bad on the grounds that I'm guilty as charged
Of breaking marsupial law?
Or did I commit this marsupial crime
For the reason I'm bad to the core?"

"If the former is true, then *you* are the one
Who is guilty of making me bad,
You should sentence yourself for making me thus,
And I should walk free and be glad."

"If the latter is true, and I'm bad to the core,
Then the guilt is not mine and not yours,
For my nature was set from the moment of birth,
Of this crime I was never the cause."

"So whatever which way that you look at this case,
It yields only one clear conclusion:
That I cannot be held to account for this crime,
For my guilt is a legal illusion."

"Clever indeed!" said the judge in reply,
"You're as sharp as a rapier sword,
But you've made one mistake in presenting your case,
Which simply can*not* be ignored."

"You say that although you committed the crime,
I've no option but let you walk free,
But isn't it true that all kangaroos jump,
Quite unable to bend at the knee?"

"That is true," said the kangaroo starting to weep,
Now crying real kangaroo tears,
"Then the option you offer is void," cried the judge,
"Your sentence is twice fifteen years!"

Clock Watching

The cold steel edge flicks
Like the blade of a knife,
And butchers the day
With cut-throat precision,
An unhurried death
By meticulous strokes,
Each a sadistically
Measured incision.

The sensitive movement
Is deftly exquisite,
This merchant of death
Has the hands of a priest,
Crossing and joining
In thanksgiving prayer,
For the flesh and the blood
Of its blasphemous feast.

Train Ride

Over the tracks,
Clickety clack,
Speeding through tunnels
Where everything's black.

Some people sleeping
And others daydreaming,
The lullaby rhythm's
What everyone's feeling,
Then into the sunlight
That's suddenly blinding
And seeing the countryside
Slowly unwinding.

Over the tracks,
Clickety clack,
Straight over bridges
With no looking back.

Small children running
Past ticket guards swaying,
And families bringing out
Board games for playing,
Businessmen making
Important decisions,
And doctors and housewives
And budding musicians,
All of them strangers
So close in position,
And all of them moving
At speed with precision.

Over the tracks,
Clickety clack,
Racing through cities
With tall chimney stacks.

Mysterious sounds
Fading into the distance,
Diminishing noises
With ghostly persistence,
Whistles and klaxons
And hoots strangely mingle
With warning bells
Somewhere outside
As they jingle,
Carriages creak on
Steel rails crunching shingle,
Fast oncoming trains
Shock your nerves
To a tingle.

Over the tracks,
Clickety clack
Rushing past fencing
Not seeing a crack.

Above all the noise
Of the talk and elation
Of passengers reaching
Their home destination
Announcements are heard
Giving cold information,
The train is approaching
Its terminus station.

Over the tracks,
Clickety clack,
Brakes are applied
And the speed is pulled back.

We struggle and rummage
To gather our luggage
And queue up ungainly
To step off the carriage,
Pulling in grandly
And slowing its motion
The train kills it movement
The doors all fly open.

Over the tracks,
Clickety clack,
The train ride is over,
We're glad to be back!

The Secret Life of the Fruit Bowl

INTRODUCTION

The world of the fruit bowl is deeply mysterious,
A world quite unknown to the chefs gastronomical,
A world best described as a citric-sweet tapestry,
A world lived in segments with zest astronomical!

From oranges, melons, sultanas and figs,
Sweet mangos, bananas and limes,
To pineapples, strawberries, cherries and plums,
Each fruit has its own life and times!

So listen to all of the fruits of the bowl,
Before they succumb to the knife,
Their secretive world is a joy to behold,
A soufflé surprise of a life!

I: FRUIT BOWL PANIC

On a table in the kitchen stands a bowl,
A red one with a pattern black as coal,
A bowl that's really lived in,
Not by rats, mice or a chicken,
But by fruit all piled up trying not to roll.

At the top there's a banana on its own,
Underneath which are four apples fully grown,
Then dates and figs and lemons,
Juicy plums and baby melons,
All are ripe but some are simply quite unknown.

The fruit begin to talk about their fate,
"I think we're fit for eating," says a date,
"Imagine being eaten,
Bitten, chewed or even beaten!"
Says a plum who joined the bowl a little late.

"I don't believe it even for a minute,"
Says a fig whose leaf begins to twitch and fidget,
"It's the colours in our skin
That make our owner laugh and grin,
Not our tasty flesh, so plum, you're wrong, admit it!"

The banana listened well to all the rumble,
Then made this speech, though he himself was humble:
"A fruit that's never eaten,
For its goodness or to sweeten,
Is a fool, so look forward to the crumble!"

II: I, TOMATO

Why, oh why, is it no-one believes me,
When I say I'm a fruit to my core?
Why, oh why, does the world misperceive me
As a vegetable brute, nothing more?

How I yearn for a high-pectin romance
With a sweet Argentinean peach,
Where we'd dance up a hot saucy salsa,
But such dreams are way way out of reach.

For I'm forced to make vegetable small-talk
With potatoes and carrots and beans,
As their rough filthy skins cut and bruise me
In a basket that nobody cleans.

How I long for the pure crystal fruit bowl,
With the oranges, apples and dates,
Where my smooth crimson skin would be treasured,
And at last I'd be one with my mates.

I belong in a rainbow fruit cocktail,
Not a dish either veggie or salady,
Will no-one release me and save me
From this heart-breaking misnomer malady?

I, Tomato here state my credentials,
Hear my warning as birthright I claim:
You may happily dice me with garlic,
But with you, to the end, lies the shame!

III: THE FRUIT BOWL BALL

One grapevine decked the hall with bunches at the Fruit Bowl Ball.

Two lemons cha-cha-d up and down, then crashed into a wall.

Three damsons danced a jiggedy-jig with a hop and a skip and a jump.

Four peaches rumba-d cheek to cheek then fell down with a bump.

Five cherries did the Hokey Kokey moving in and out,

And when they'd finished dancing they all shook themselves about!

IV: THE BALLAD OF THE RASPBERRY CRUSH

The heart-throb of the fruit bowl enthralled her,
She had fallen for him from the start,
The shy little raspberry was smitten,
The passion-fruit had stolen her heart.

She adored his exotic complexion,
His aroma was heavenly bliss,
If only he knew how she loved him,
How her dreams were consumed with his kiss.

The passion-fruit heart-throb was dashing,
A travelled and wit raconteur,
The raspberry felt less than useless,
Why should *he* seek out romance with *her*?

Cupid's arrow had struck and condemned her
To a rapture that made her forlorn,
Of feeling alive for the very first time,
Yet wishing she'd never been born.

Inconsolable, desperate and weary,
She was love-sick and wasting away,
She had lost all her raspberry ripple,
She now dreaded the dawn of each day.

So one terrible night in the fruit bowl,
With the passion-fruit's name on her breath,
The raspberry climbed to the rim of the bowl,
And
fell
fell
fell
fell
fell
fell
to
her
death.

V: OLYMPIC FRUIT BOWL

The fruits were lined up for a race all waiting for the off,

But they jumped the gun and ran ahead on hearing Mango cough.

The Spanish melon got a stitch and fell down with a thud,

The French grape slid along the ground and scooped up all the mud.

The Turkish currant tried to fly and hit a passing cloud,

The English cherry lost his way and rolled into the crowd.

The Greek fig tried no fancy tricks but kept a steady pace,

And smoothly passed the finish tape to win the fruit bowl race.

VI: HIS EXCELLENCY THE EMPEROR LYCHEE OF CHINA AND HIS TREACHEROUS MANDARINS

"May you live in interesting times!"
Boomed the Emperor Lychee of China
As his mandarins bowed in prostration
And his mood turned from major to minor.

"I am sick of your fawning corruption!
For your treachery now you will pay!
I've commissioned this timepiece to govern you
And enslave you each night and each day!"

The emperor unveiled the new clock,
Its face had five hands in a wreath,
It was mounted on five golden dragons,
And each one held five bells in its teeth.

"You will notice the clock has no numbers
Which means that it tells not the time,
But when started it rings out five times every day,
And each set of five bells sounds a chime."

"Each hand stands for one Chinese element:
Earth, Water, Fire, Wood and Air,
And depending on which dragon rings out the chime
Will determine your task, so beware!"

"For Earth you must eat five dry handfuls of dust,
For Fire five hot coals must you seize,
For Water you must dive down five fathoms of sea,
For Wood you must fell five tall trees."

"For Air you must capture the pure mountain breeze,
And bring it to earth in five jars,
Thus the clock will enslave you with five dreadful tasks,
Like a prison without any bars!"

"The Emperor Lychee has spoken!
Let our words now be written by scribes,
The mandarins now have their punishment,
For their treason, corruption and bribes."

The mandarins begged for forgiveness
As the clock was set ticking in motion,
But the emperor walked out unmoved
As his silken robes waved like the ocean.

The mandarins fearful and trembling,
Now awaited the first of the chimes,
The emperor's strange curse was upon them:
They were living in interesting times!

VII: STRAWBERRY COUP

They arrived in a grey cardboard punnet,
Those imposters with seed-pocked-marked skin,
Their plan was so perfect: a fruit bowl whodunit,
Pulled off by the strawberries within.

They rapidly rose to a status supreme,
And just nobody gave it a thought,
As champagne flowed in magnums with rich clotted cream,
On Wimbledon's prized Centre Court.

But a fruit has to have all its seeds packed within,
Not outside all on show like a rash on the skin,
So the strawbs all climbed high on a claim wafer-thin,
For as fruits they're as fake as a Cheshire Cat's grin!

Their jet-setting lifestyle of glamour and glitz
Cast the rest of the fruit bowl in shade,
They dined at the best: the Savoy and the Ritz,
They were loved; they'd arrived; they were made.

They followed the money, each romance and kiss,
As they conquered the World batch by batch,
They reeked of success and sheer culinary bliss,
An edible game, set and match!

Unwritten Letter from a Statue to the Artist

How did you know I existed?
How did you know I was there,
Waiting for ever to meet you
Inside that grey stone cold and bare?

What methods were used to divine me?
Did you listen to oracles speak?
What signals and trails did you follow?
Just how did you know where to seek?

How did you find me from nothing?
What magical spells did you cast?
Did you draw up new maps for direction?
Or decipher lost codes that you passed?

Did mystical sages advise you?
Were you given a new compass rose?
How on earth did you come by the knowledge
That it was you – no-one else – whom I chose?

These secrets may never be yielded
To scholars who struggle and strive,
But no matter, for I am now with you,
And somehow through love, I'm alive.

The Author

I have at my wanton disposal
Secret weapons of mass destruction,
After many long years of hard research,
I have perfected their deadly construction,
I can fire them at will without warning
From silos that are hidden from sight,
And once launched, they evade all detection
Since they travel on the wavelength of light,
They vary in size and in compass
According to plan and design,
But all are pre-programmed and targeted
And, once primed, they're no longer benign.

Although each one explodes upon impact,
These weapons are far from conventional,
For their structure is purely linguistic,
And their deployment is always intentional,
Each weapon is known as a SENTENCE,
But one that is perfectly crafted
Out of words all syntactically structured
Into a meaning exquisitely drafted,
Every sentence is quite individual,
No two are exactly the same,
But that does not mean that they cannot be grouped
By classification and name:

Positive sentences, negative sentences,
Sentences major and minor,
Sentences stately in phrasing and cadence,
Sentences fit for Regina,
Comical sentences, serious sentences,
Sentences short and laconic,
Sentences complex in concept and grammar,
Sentences wry and sardonic,
Tactical sentences, pivotal sentences,
Sentences giving instruction,
Embarrassing sentences curling each toe,
Sentences causing a ruction,
Valedictory sentences, scholarly sentences,
Sentences sly and mendacious,
Sentences heartfelt and gently romantic,
Sentences subtle and gracious,
Revolutionary sentences, frightening sentences,
Sentences shocking and frantic,
Sentences aimed at commencement of conflict,
Sentences mystically tantric,
Factual sentences, fictional sentences,
Sentences scrawled as graffiti,
Sentences pensive and darkly implosive,
Sentences begging entreaty,
Mellifluous sentences, quizzical sentences,
Sentences morally loaded,
Sentences building to great peroration,
Sentences cryptically coded,
Inscrutable sentences, visceral sentences,
Sentences bold and dramatic,
Sentences cutting and coldly forensic,
Sentences wildly ecstatic,
Definitive sentences, mischievous sentences,
Sentences quite pedagogical,
Sentences dealing with things legalistic,
Sentences strangely illogical,

Particular sentences, general sentences,
Sentences pious and prayerful,
Sentences riddled with riotous rhymes,
Sentences patiently careful,
Paranoid sentences, magical sentences,
Sentences all metaphorical,
Sentences rhythmic in tempo and pulse,
Sentences phantasmagorical!

Now why, you might ask, is a sentence a weapon
When weapons are purely destructive?
Well, the answer is simple and easy to grasp,
And like all truths profoundly instructive,
When the form of a sentence is perfectly honed
Through patient semantic endeavour,
Its delivery can blast the dumb state of the world
With shockwaves that travel for ever,
A well-crafted sentence can topple dictators
Or reduce populations to laughter,
A sentence can uproot the deepest beliefs
And transform human life ever after,
A finely tuned sentence in meaning and structure
Can shatter the oldest of rules,
A sentence can turn the whole world upside-down,
Or vaporise unwitting fools.

So beware of my arsenal of weapons,
I am not to be mocked or ignored,
Like a Greek god on Great Mount Olympus,
I'm capricious and easily bored,
I am the maker and destroyer of worlds,
I control every heartbeat and breath,
My sentences give me the ultimate power:
I am the keeper of life and of death.

Alchemy

The sculptor chips stone into form,
The painter turns oil into light,
The dancer translates every language to movement,
The lawyer discerns wrong from right.

The writer distils life from ink,
The athlete makes fluid the race,
The clockmaker measures invisible moments,
The architect captures the space.

The tailor cuts cloth into style,
The gardener fashions the ground,
The cartographer scales down the world to a ball,
The composer makes journeys through sound.

The cook whips up food into flavour,
The cleaner buffs old into new,
The scientist abstracts hidden patterns and laws,
The actor becomes me and you.

So abandon your dallies with magic,
Such hokum is lifeless and cold,
Real alchemy lies all around you,
Transforming the world into gold.